Becoming a Star Teacher

Becoming a Star Teacher

Practical Strategies and Inspiration for K-6 Teachers

Patricia M. Hart
James B. Rowley

CORWIN PRESS, INC.
A Sage Publications Company
Thousand Oaks, California

Copyright © 1997 by Corwin Press, Inc.

All rights reserved. No part of this book may be reproduced or utilized in any form or by any means, electronic or mechanical, including photocopying, recording, or by any information storage and retrieval system, without permission in writing from the publisher.

For information address:

Corwin Press, Inc.
A Sage Publications Company
2455 Teller Road
Thousand Oaks, California 91320
E-mail: order@corwin.sagepub.com

SAGE Publications Ltd.
6 Bonhill Street
London EC2A 4PU
United Kingdom

SAGE Publications India Pvt. Ltd.
M-32 Market
Greater Kailash I
New Delhi 110 048 India

ISBN 0-8039-6685-7

This book is printed on acid-free paper.

97 98 99 00 01 10 9 8 7 6 5 4 3 2 1

Corwin Press Production Editor: S. Marlene Head

Contents

PREFACE	vii
Alternate Uses	vii
Program Contents Described	viii
Acknowledgments	x
ABOUT THE DEVELOPERS	xi
ABOUT THE TEACHERS	xii
INTRODUCTION	1
How to Use This Program	1
CHAPTER 1 TEACHER AS DECISION MAKER	3
Decision Making: An Imperfect Process	4
Correcting a Decision	5
Seeking Wise Counsel	6
Veteran Advice	7
References	8
CHAPTER 2 TEACHER AS COMMUNITY BUILDER	10
The School Community	11
Student Expectations	12
The Ideal Classroom Community	13
Veteran Advice	14
References	15
CHAPTER 3 TEACHER AS MANAGER	17
Classroom Management Checklist	18
Hugs and Bugs	19
Reaching Every Student	20
Documentation	21
Veteran Advice	23
References	24

CHAPTER 4   TEACHER AS CURRICULUM DEVELOPER   26

    Curriculum Development Inventory   27
    Inventory Results   28
    Motivation to Learn   29
    Lesson-Planning Survey   30
    Sample Planning Format   31
    Veteran Advice   34
    References   35

CHAPTER 5   TEACHER AS COUNSELOR   38

    Warning Signs   39
    Learning Through Observation   40
    The Next Step   41
    Veteran Advice   42
    References   43

CHAPTER 6   TEACHER AS EVALUATOR   45

    Completing the Picture   46
    Planning the Path   47
    Family Conference Tips   48
    Veteran Advice   49
    References   50

CHAPTER 7   TEACHER AS DIVERSITY SPECIALIST   52

    Gift List   53
    Self-Evaluation   54
    Celebrating Diversity   55
    I Am Special   56
    Veteran Advice   57
    References   58

CHAPTER 8   THE JOYS OF TEACHING   60

    Shining Star   61
    Secrets of Success   62
    Summer Contract   63
    A Year in Review   64
    Veteran Advice   65
    References   66

Preface

Many first-year teachers, despite their desire to function as autonomous professionals, soon recognize they are in need of guidance and support. Depending on the nature and severity of the problems encountered, different types of help are required. In some cases, appropriate information or strategic advice is called for, whereas in other cases emotional support and understanding are equally or more important. Fortunately, many school districts now have formalized support programs that rely on veteran teachers to serve as mentors for entry-year teachers. Although having a committed and caring mentor can make a tremendous difference, the first year of teaching can remain a challenging and sometimes lonely experience.

Becoming a Star Teacher: Practical Strategies and Inspiration for K-6 Teachers was created to provide beginning teachers with convenient access to the wisdom of four outstanding teachers with over 50 combined years of K-6 experience. The eight audiotapes and workbook that comprise the program were not designed to substitute for the services of a mentor teacher. In fact, they were developed to support the work of mentors as well as beginning teachers. As experienced mentor teachers well know, there is great power in shared experience and the opportunities such experience provides for self-disclosure, trust building, and collegial dialogue. Each of the eight audiotapes and accompanying workbook activities in this program serve as powerful opportunities for such shared experience.

Alternate Uses

Becoming a Star Teacher: Practical Strategies and Inspiration for K-6 Teachers can be used in a variety of professional development settings. In addition to being used by individual teachers as a source of technical and emotional support, the program also works well in the context of entry-year support programs. In those schools or districts where entry-year teachers meet with support personnel throughout the school year, the tapes and workbook activities can serve as the stimuli for small-group dialogue and reflection. In addition, the same materials can be effectively employed by mentor or protege teams as a vehicle for promoting personal discussion of a wide variety of topics and issues of importance to veteran as well as beginning teachers.

Building administrators may also put the programs to effective use by employing them as professional development resources they can provide to beginning teachers interested in, or needing help with, one of the areas covered on the tapes. University-based teacher educators can also make use of the program as a vehicle for bringing the wisdom of veteran teachers to the preservice classroom. Because they focus on the first year of teaching, the audiotapes and workbook exercises transfer well to beginning teachers working in student teaching or other clinical settings.

Program Contents Described

Much has been written in the past decade about the need to promote teacher reflection. Similarly, there have been repeated calls to find new ways to bring teacher voice to the professional development process. Clearly, outstanding veteran practitioners such as those featured in this program can be powerful forces in helping novice teachers make the theory-to-practice connections that help define professional practice. Delivering teacher voice via audiotape places teacher knowledge in the hands of the beginner to be accessed whenever desired or needed.

One of the reasons classroom teaching is such a challenging profession is that teachers are continually called on to perform a variety of tasks requiring wide-ranging skills and deep knowledge. This program captures the complexity of teaching by advancing seven *images* of the professional teacher ranging from *Teacher as Community Builder* to *Teacher as Diversity Specialist*. Each program is tailored to address a different professional problem frequently encountered by beginning teachers. For example, help with the problem of planning classwork is found in *Teacher as Curriculum Developer* and the problem of dealing with students' personal problems is addressed in *Teacher as Counselor*. In addition to providing the wisdom of practice of veteran teachers via audiotape, beginning teachers are encouraged to reflect on their own practice by completing workbook activities designed to support and extend the audiotape material.

In the opening program, listeners are introduced to the four classroom teachers who serve as the electronic mentors throughout the series. In addition, they also meet the two university-based teacher educators who alternate in facilitating the eight audio discussions. Following introductions, the topic of *Teacher as Decision Maker* is introduced and discussed as an organizing theme for the remaining programs.

The next six audiotapes are each devoted to alternate images of professional practice. *Teacher as Community Builder* provides specific advice on how to build community spirit with parents, staff, and students. Working to build a community of learners is described as being fundamentally important to the teaching and learning process, and beginning teachers are inspired to begin the process from the first day of the school year.

In *Teacher as Manager*, attention turns to the business of learning to manage space, time, materials, and student behavior. Practical suggestions on how to develop and communicate daily routines are among the topics covered. The program ends with the teachers discussing the importance of teachers learning to manage their own lives so they can maintain positive outlooks and personal energy.

Designing and delivering engaging instruction is the focus of *Teacher as Curriculum Developer*. In this program, beginning teachers learn how veteran teachers have found success in this area through reading, belonging to professional organizations, and networking with colleagues. Practical strategies for planning are also discussed.

Dealing with students' personal problems can be a particularly challenging task for beginning teachers. *Teacher as Counselor* focuses on this area by having the veteran teachers share cases from their own experience as vehicles for helping beginning teachers gain insight not only on some of the key principles that guide them in their work with children but also the diversity of problems they often carry with them to school.

In *Teacher as Evaluator*, the veteran teachers discuss the important topic of student evaluation and the need for teachers to develop a broader repertoire of assessment strategies. In addition to describing their personal evolution in this area of professional development, the teachers remind listeners of the importance of setting clear expectations for students and being fair and consistent in their evaluation of student work.

Recognizing, accepting, and celebrating the many differences that characterize the lives of students is the topic of *Teacher as Diversity Specialist*.

Meeting students' individual needs is discussed from a variety of perspectives. This program encourages beginning teachers to promote a classroom climate and culture that welcomes all students as capable learners.

In the final program, *The Joys of Teaching*, the four teachers describe how classroom teaching has been a source of fulfillment in their personal lives. In addition to discussing the various ways that teaching has contributed to their quality of life, Joni, Judy, Rhonda, and Steve offer specific suggestions for maintaining positive attitudes and a high level of commitment to one's profession.

Acknowledgments

This program was made possible with the support of many people, including Jackie Marshall Arnold, graduate research assistant at the University of Dayton, who provided important technical and editorial support throughout the project. Thanks are also extended to Angie Haines, elementary teacher in the Northmont, Ohio Schools, who helped in the initial design of the workbook activities, and to David Lesko of Lesko Photography for taking the portraits of the participants in the series. Ann Raney of the University of Dayton's Curriculum Materials Center and Terri Stringer of the Dayton and Montgomery County public library system provided valued assistance in the development of the reference section that concludes each workbook chapter. Eric Johnson of Educational Video Publishing deserves special thanks for his work as producer and editor of the audio programs and for his much-appreciated support of the project from its earliest conception to completion.

Finally, our respect and appreciation are extended to the four veteran teachers who made this program possible: Joni Edmondson, Judy Eggemeier, Rhonda Mumaw, and Steve Huff. Thank you for so openly and thoughtfully sharing your wisdom of practice.

Patricia M. Hart & James B. Rowley
Dayton, Ohio

About the Developers

Becoming a Star Teacher: Practical Strategies and Inspiration for K-6 Teachers was created and coproduced by Patricia M. Hart and James B. Rowley, associate professors of education at the University of Dayton. Other professional development programs produced by Tricia and Jim include the video-based training programs *Mentoring the New Teacher* (1993) and *Becoming a Star Urban Teacher* (1995). Jim and Tricia are dedicated to using electronic media to capture and communicate the knowledge and wisdom of classroom teachers. In 1993, and again in 1995, Jim and Tricia received the Distinguished Research in Teacher Education award presented annually by the national Association of Teacher Educators (ATE).

About the Teachers

Joni Edmondson teaches first grade at Valley Forge Elementary in the Huber Heights, Ohio school district. Joni has been teaching for 25 years.

Judy Eggemeier teaches sixth grade at Southdale Elementary in the Kettering-Moraine, Ohio school district. Judy has been teaching for 15 years.

Steve Huff teaches fifth grade at Cline Elementary in the Centerville, Ohio school district. Steve has been teaching for 7 years.

Rhonda Mumaw teaches third grade at Southdale Elementary in the Kettering-Moraine, Ohio school district. Rhonda has been teaching for 8 years.

Introduction

Welcome to *Becoming a Star Teacher: Practical Strategies and Inspiration for K-6 Teachers.* It is our hope that the eight audiotapes and workbook that comprise this program will be sources of support and inspiration as you meet the important challenges of your first year of teaching. We trust that you will have the support of a formal or informal mentor teacher as you begin your professional career. Whether or not you are so fortunate, we are confident that you will find valuable advice and invaluable wisdom in the voices of the veteran teachers you will come to know throughout the eight audiotape programs.

If you do not have a mentor teacher to turn to for collegial support, we hope that you will come to think of Joni, Judy, Rhonda, and Steve as a mentoring team dedicated to helping you succeed in the important work you have chosen to pursue. If you have a mentor teacher, we encourage you to share this program with him or her so that the two of you might use the tapes and this workbook as springboards to even deeper conversations about teaching and learning in the elementary grades.

How to Use This Program

We suggest that you begin by listening to Tape 1: *Introductions and Teacher as Decision Maker*. In this program you will be introduced to Joni Edmondson, Judy Eggemeier, Steve Huff, and Rhonda Mumaw, the four veteran teachers whose wisdom of practice is the heart of this series. After the introductions, you will listen in as the teachers share their insights on *Teacher as Decision Maker*. The remaining seven programs have been structured to reflect the order in which they might be needed by a beginning teacher. This structure, however, is not critical because each of the remaining tapes constitute a stand-alone program. Consequently, you may prefer to listen to whatever tape you feel best meets your needs at a given time. Whatever method you employ, we know you will profit from returning to the tapes for repeated listening.

Every audiotape program in the series is supported by a section in this workbook. Each corresponding section has been designed to help you reflect on and apply the many suggestions offered by the veteran teachers. We suggest that after listening to each tape you turn to the appropriate workbook section and complete the activities related to that program.

In addition to the three or more activities that comprise each section, you will find a summary of the key pieces of advice put forth by Joni, Judy, Rhonda, and Steve. Finally, you will find references at the end of each section that provides bibliographic information for the professional books and children's literature referred to in the audio program. In addition, you will also find references for other books that may be valuable resources related to the topics and issues discussed in that program.

The final tape in the series is titled *The Joys of Teaching*. In bringing closure, Joni, Judy, Rhonda, and Steve share their personal stories as classroom teachers and describe the special meaning teaching has brought to their respective lives. We think you will be inspired by the commitment and optimism that characterize these veteran practitioners and hope that their thoughts will help guide you to a successful first year and a joyful career.

Teacher as Decision Maker

As John Dewey reminds us, "Prize the doubt." Problem solving often begins in a state of confusion and uncertainty.

-Jim Rowley

Teacher as Decision Maker

Decision Making: An Imperfect Process

At times, the role of decision maker can seem a little overwhelming for beginning teachers. Numerous studies have concluded that classroom teachers make hundreds of decisions every school day. Joni, Judy, Rhonda, and Steve agree that this task becomes easier with experience. However, they also admit that despite their experience, they still make some less-than-perfect decisions. Accepting fallibility as a decision maker is an important step in your professional growth. The purpose of the following activity is to promote reflection on a couple of important decisions you have made recently.

These are two of the strong decisions I have made:

1. _____
   _____

2. _____
   _____

These are two decisions I wish I had handled differently:

1. _____
   _____

2. _____
   _____

Teacher as Decision Maker

Correcting a Decision

Because you are a fallible human being and will make mistakes, it is important to realize that a decision can in many cases be reversed or corrected. The purpose of this activity is to help you reflect on how you can recover from a difficult decision. The first step in the process is the awareness that you were responsible for the decision and its negative consequences. After describing the decision in the box below, reflect on the questions that follow.

Briefly describe the decision and why you feel it has had negative consequences.

1. Did I make this decision only after attempting to take the other person(s) point of view?

2. Have I apologized to the person(s) involved?

3. What can I do to correct the situation?

4. What could I do differently the next time a similar situation arises?

5. What have I learned from this situation?

Teacher as Decision Maker

Seeking Wise Counsel

Jim introduced the notion that teachers make different kinds of decisions. Some are pre-active, some are post-active, and many are interactive. Although you frequently will not have the time to consult with other professionals when making the interactive decisions that occur during the instructional process, you will have the time to do so on many other important decisions. As you think about who to consult regarding a professional decision, consider the following guidelines. Then conclude by listing the names of three people who qualify as good people to turn to for advice and support.

Qualifying Questions

- Does the person have a personal or professional interest in me or in the situation I am encountering?

- Does the person have knowledge and experience relative to the decision I am trying to make?

- Is the person trustworthy?

- Will the person be willing to tell me what I need to hear, even if it is something I may not want to hear?

People Who Qualify to Help Me

1. _____

2. _____

3. _____

Teacher as Decision Maker

Advice From Joni, Judy, Rhonda, and Steve

* Ask yourself, "What is best for this child?"

* Run your thoughts by someone else--get a second opinion.

* When appropriate, involve students in decisions that include them.

* Do not rush into making a serious decision.

* Think through your decisions. Make sure you have all the accurate information needed.

* Consult your administrators for advice. They have the experience to know what to do in many particular situations.

* Reflect on your decisions, and remember, you are allowed to change your mind.

* Take risks.

* Trust yourself. You are a professional.

References for
Teacher as Decision Maker

Professional Reading

Calderhead, J. (1984). *Teachers' Classroom Decision Making.* Holt, Rinehart & Winston.

Dewey, John. (1910). *How We Think.* D. C. Heath & Co.

Jonson, Kathleen. (1997). *The New Elementary Teachers' Handbook: (Almost) Everything You Need to Know for Your First Years of Teaching.* Corwin Press.

Langer, G. M., & Colton, A. B. (1994). Reflective Decision Making: The Cornerstone of School Reform. *Journal of Staff Development, 15*(1), 2-7.

McCarney, S. B., Wunderlich, K. C., & Bauer, A. M. (1994). *The Teacher's Resource Guide.* Hawthorne Educational Services.

Moran, Carrol, et al. (1992). *Keys to the Classroom: A Teacher's Guide to the First Month of School.* Corwin Press.

Pasch, M. (1995). *Teaching as Decision Making: Successful Practices for the Elementary Teacher.* Longman.

Rosenblum-Lowden, Renee. (1997). *"You Have to Go to School...You're the Teacher!" 200 Tips to Make Your Job Easier and More Fun.* Corwin Press.

Strohmer, Joanne, & Carhart, Clare. (1997). *Time-Saving Tips for Teachers.* Corwin Press.

Children's Literature

Arnosky, Jim. (1991). *The Empty Lot.* Little, Brown and Co. Perspective plays such a critical role in how you "see" a situation. This dimension plays a part in our main character's decision of whether to sell or keep his "empty" lot.

Buckley, Helen. (1994). *Grandfather and I.* Lothrop, Lee & Shepard. "Decide" to "never hurry" your children and listen to them as they spend the school year with you.

Cole, W. (1983). *Poem Stew*. Trophy Press. An anthology of poems to add to your collection. Steve is introduced in the audio series reading a poem from this exciting book.

Ehlert, Lois. (1994). *Mole's Hill*. Harcourt Brace & Company. Mole's good thinking saves his home from destruction and ultimately benefits all members of this community.

Lindbergh, Reeve. (1996). *Nobody Owns the Sky*. Candlewick Press. This well-written biography of Bessie Coleman, the famous African American pilot, reinforces for all readers the idea that you are in control of your own life. Determination and belief in her abilities were the foundation of a decision she made early in her life that influenced her career decision.

Polacco, Patricia. (1991). *Applemando's Dream*. Philomel. Applemando thought a little differently than the other members of his community. Finally, after people decided to view his thinking with a more open attitude, he was appreciated for the gifts he had to offer everyone.

Teacher as Community Builder

Community building is the most important thing we do as teachers. It sets the tone for the parents, the staff, and certainly the students.

-Judy Eggemeier

Teacher as Community Builder

The School Community

Joni, Judy, Rhonda, and Steve stressed the importance of modeling respect for all professionals in your school. They suggested calling these people by name and sending thank-you notes from the class if and when appropriate. In order to do so, it is necessary to learn each person's name. As a first-year teacher, use this sheet to help you remember the name of each of the members of your school community.

Principal	_____	Librarian	_____
Vice Principal	_____	Library Assistant	_____
Secretary	_____	Technology Coor.	_____
Secretary	_____	Cafeteria Worker	_____
Nurse	_____	Cafeteria Worker	_____
Psychologist	_____	Speech Therapist	_____
Janitor	_____	Resource Room	_____
Janitor	_____	Resource Room	_____
Teacher's Aid	_____	Resource Room	_____
Teacher's Aid	_____	Resource Room	_____
Teacher's Aid	_____	Physical Education	_____
Volunteer	_____	Music Teacher	_____
Volunteer	_____	Art Teacher	_____

Teacher as Community Builder

Student Expectations

Steve talked about the survey he distributes to his fifth-grade class each year. Two simple questions help him build community in his class with his students because their responses allow him to discover what they expect from him. This type of survey works well with older students. In the younger grades, it might be more effective to discuss these questions as a class. After you have studied the survey responses or reflected on your class discussion, complete the following outlines. Throughout the school year, periodically return to this page to review your performance in light of *student expectations*.

My students think a good teacher . . .

1.

2.

3.

4.

My students think a poor teacher . . .

1.

2.

3.

4.

Teacher as Community Builder

The Ideal Classroom Community

Steve, Rhonda, Judy, and Joni talk throughout this program about the importance of building a classroom community among your students. Below is a list of ideas that you could implement to help strengthen the community that is within your classroom walls. Check below the strategies that you have used to develop a sense of community in your room. Consider employing those strategies you have not tried. Remember:

A community is . . .

1. A group of people living in the same locality under the same government

2. A social group having common interests

Ways to Develop Community

- _____ Model respect.
- _____ Mutually develop class rules.
- _____ Invite student input in room arrangement.
- _____ Employ activities that allow you and your students to get to know each other personally.
- _____ Create an activity early in the year that requires teamwork.
- _____ Employ cooperative learning strategies.
- _____ Praise behaviors that exemplify good citizenship.
- _____ Develop class pride through common goals, logos, mottos, and so forth.
- _____ Invite students to collaborate and develop class goals.
- _____ Encourage and expect appropriate manners from the children.
- _____ See each child as an individual learner.
- _____ Develop positive relationships with and support from the parents and families of the students you teach.
- _____ Use a calm and kind voice.
- _____ Use literature and the curriculum to integrate the theme of respect.

Teacher as Community Builder

Advice From Joni, Judy, Rhonda, and Steve

Building Community With Parents

* Send a cheerful note home to parents before the school year starts.

* Make positive phone calls home every now and then.

* Ask parents to write letters to you about their child.

Building Community With Staff

* Make friends with the janitors, secretaries, and cafeteria workers.

* Eat lunch with the other teachers. Learn from them and be social with them.

Building Community With Students

* Give the students a survey that gives them the opportunity to share their ideas about teaching.

* Be careful when you raise your voice. Students remember these moments.

* Make sure your students know that each day is a new day. So if they angered you on Monday, you will forget about it by Tuesday.

* Make community building a part of your curriculum at the beginning of each year. There are many ways it can be tied in to other subjects.

* Let the students know you are a real person with some of the same interests they have. Tell them about your hobbies. Let them know you are a learner just like they are.

* Show the children you respect them.

* Remember that community building is a gradual process.

References for Teacher as Community Builder

Professional Reading

Calkins, L. (1991). *Living Between the Lines*. Heinemann.

Canter, L., & Petersen, K. (1995). *Teaching Students to Get Along*. Lee Canter and Associates.

Davis, G. (1996). *Teaching Values: An Idea Book for Teachers (and Parents)*. Westwood.

Duggan, Mary Anne. (1997). *Powerful Parent Letters for K-3*. Corwin Press.

Harwayne, S. (1992). *Lasting Impressions*. Heinemann.

Hopkins, S., & Winters, J (Eds.). (1990). *Discover the World: Empowering Children to Value Themselves, Others and the Earth*. New Society.

Kreidler, W. (1995). We're All in This Together: Fun-Filled Games That Promote Community. *Instructor, 105*(3), 24-25.

Lasley, T. (1994). *Teaching Peace*. Bergin & Garvey.

Warner, Carolyn. (1997). *Everybody's House--The Schoolhouse: Best Techniques for Connecting Home, School, and Community*. Corwin Press.

Children's Literature

Blos, Joan. (1987). *Old Henry*. Mulberry. This simple picture book conveys the message clearly about the value of acceptance and compromise.

Cannon, Janell. (1993). *Stellaluna*. Harcourt Brace & Co. A heart-warming story of a fruit bat raised by a bird family. In the end, the final discussion says it all when the birds and the bats discuss their differences and conclude that those differences are not important. What matters is that they care for each other and are friends.

dePaola, Tomie. (1983). *The Legend of the Bluebonnet*. Scholastic. A Native American legend that raises the question of how much a person will sacrifice for the good of the larger community.

Fox, Mem. (1985). *Wilfrid Gordon McDonald Partridge*. Kane/Miller. Through the kindness and generous spirit of Wilfrid, the young main character, his best friend Miss Nancy "regains" her memory.

Freedman, Florence. (1985). *Brothers*. Harper & Row. A Hebrew legend about the selfless love of two brothers.

Lester, Helen. (1988). *Tacky the Penguin*. Houghton Mifflin. A fun story with the vital message to respect and accept the "Tackys" in the world.

Pulver, Robin. (1990). *Mrs. Toggle's Zipper*. Four Winds. The "whole" school community works together to unzip Mrs. Toggle's stuck zipper.

Teacher as Manager

An artist's studio, while it is set up for creativity, has a certain structure and often that structure is very simple.

—Rhonda Mumaw

Teacher as Manager

Classroom Management Checklist

The following questionnaire is based on many insights from Joni, Judy, Rhonda, and Steve, as well as on the research on effective classroom management. Read it prior to the beginning of the school year as a way of ensuring a solid start, or anytime during the year as a way of checking your performance.

Read the following statements and circle Y (Yes), N (No), or S (Sometimes).

Y N S	I have a system for handling student paperwork.
Y N S	I have a system for handling my own paperwork.
Y N S	There is plenty of designated work space for students.
Y N S	Frequently used materials are accessible.
Y N S	I know where our discipline plan will be posted.
Y N S	A copy of the class routine is available to students.
Y N S	Students have a morning task at the beginning of each day.
Y N S	The students and I have established one way in which I can always capture their attention.
Y N S	My first letter or phone call to the parents will be a positive one.
Y N S	When students are disciplined, they understand why.
Y N S	I am fair and consistent in the classroom.
Y N S	I make the students feel successful when modifying their behavior.

Teacher as Manager

Hugs and Bugs

Drawing on Rhonda's suggestion, first reflect on student behaviors that you find commendable (*hugs*) or disturbing (*bugs*). Then, ask your students, working alone or in groups, to identify their hugs and bugs. Finally, using the students' reflections and your personal thoughts, facilitate a discussion about expectations for classroom behavior. Looking at your hugs and bugs, reflect on what you do or could do to commend hugs and discourage bugs. Note: You may want to rename this activity for older students.

HUGS

1.
2.
3.
4.
5.

BUGS

1.
2.
3.
4.
5.

Teacher as Manager

Reaching Every Student

Judy mentioned that it is difficult for teachers to balance time among "high-maintenance" and "low-maintenance" students. It is important for each child in your class to feel welcome, and you never want to feel as though you have neglected a student in your classroom. About a month into the school year, use this worksheet to list certain students in your class. Set a goal for each one of them. This goal should be something that you would like to see the student do before the end of the first quarter. These goals might be academic or nonacademic in nature. Some examples might be: reading for better comprehension; being willing to take more risks in group work; or even smiling more at school.

HIGH MAINTENANCE
(students who require an inordinate amount of attention)

Student	Goal
1.	
2.	
3.	
4.	
5.	

LOW MAINTENANCE
(students who are independent achievers and require little attention from the teacher)

Student	Goal
1.	
2.	
3.	
4.	
5.	

Teacher as Manager

Documentation

Documentation and accurate record keeping are hallmarks of professionalism. Veteran classroom teachers recognize the importance of documenting student behavior patterns. In addition, many veteran teachers maintain a written record of the actions they have taken in an effort to help students change their behavior. If you are dealing with a student's challenging discipline problem, consider the following list of reasons why many experienced teachers employ documentation. On the following page, you will find a simple form that you can use as you begin to experiment with this important professional practice.

Reasons to Document:

1. To help you see patterns in student behavior

2. To help you see patterns in your own behavior

3. To collect the specific data that is critical to the problem solving process

4. To acquire the insights that can help you more accurately communicate the problem to others

5. To protect yourself from unfair claims and accusations

6. To help you reflect on the various strategies you have employed

7. To remind you of the persistence that is often required to solve challenging problems

Student Name_____ Teacher_____

Description of problem behavior: _____
_____
_____
_____
_____

ACTIONS TAKEN	DATE

Comments: _____
_____
_____

Teacher as Manager

Advice From Joni, Judy, Rhonda, and Steve

* When appropriate, involve children in classroom decisions.

* Keep your routines simple.

* Post your routines.

* Set logical consequences.

* Be consistent.

* Send a set of class rules home to parents.

* Send a set of class rules to your principal.

* Give students responsibility in helping their classroom run smoothly.

* Be ready to remind students of certain things, especially those things they do not find engaging (e.g., cleaning up at the end of the day).

* Read parenting books to help you manage your classroom.

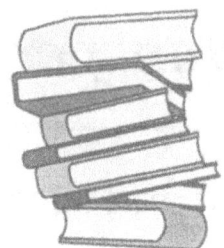

References for Teacher as Manager

Professional Reading

A to EZ Handbook: Staff Development Guide. (1993). Macmillan/McGraw-Hill.

Covey, Steven. (1990). *The Seven Habits of Highly Effective People.* Simon & Schuster.

DiGiulio, Robert. (1995). *Positive Classroom Management: A Step-by-Step Guide to Successfully Running the Show Without Destroying Student Dignity.* Corwin Press.

Gootman, Marilyn. (1997). *The Caring Teacher's Guide to Discipline: Helping Young Students Learn Self-Control, Responsibility, and Respect.* Corwin Press.

Johnson, S., & Johnson, C. (1986). *The One-Minute Teacher: How to Teach Others to Teach Themselves.* Quill/William Morrow.

Koenig, Larry. (1995). *Smart Discipline for the Classroom: Respect and Cooperation Restored* (Revised ed.). Corwin Press.

Kottler, Jeffrey. (1997). *Success With Challenging Students.* Corwin Press.

Schell, L. M., & Burden, P. (1992). *Countdown to the First Day of School.* National Education Association.

Schwartz, S., & Pollishuke, M. (1991). *Creating the Child-Centered Classroom.* Richard C. Owens.

Children's Literature

Brady, Kimberley. (1996). *Keeper for the Sea.* Simon & Schuster. "And I remember even fisherman have rules." To be effective, there are rules to follow, and this book shares with the reader rules for being successful at fishing.

Cazet, Denys. (1990). *Never Spit on Your Shoes.* Orchard. This clever book follows Arnie through his first day of first grade where the children contribute to the classroom rules. The book is written from a first grader's perspective, which adds to the humor in the day.

Murphy, Jill. (1986). *Five Minutes' Peace*. B. P. Putnam. A good manager ensures that he or she has time alone throughout a busy day.

Steig, William (1986). *Brave Irene*. Farrar, Straus and Giroux. Classroom management requires persistence, and Irene is a wonderful example of persistence in her endeavor in this book.

Zimelman, Nathan. (1992). *How the Second Grade Got $8,205.50 to Visit the Statue of Liberty*. Albert Whitman & Co. One aspect of managing as a teacher is to incorporate humor into your life. Read this book and enjoy a visit with a very ambitious second grade.

Teacher as Curriculum Developer

School should be life. It should be a place where students come to share the excitement of living and learning together.

—Rhonda Mumaw

Teacher as Curriculum Developer

Curriculum Development Inventory

Joni described the importance of improving on one area of the curriculum at a time. Under each heading rate yourself on a scale of 1-10, with 1 being *weak* and 10 being *strong*. Then, add your scores going across and record the total. After reviewing your scores, begin to generate ideas on how you can create more of an instructional balance in your classroom.

Personal Knowledge: How much do I know about this subject? How comfortable am I teaching the concepts in this subject area? Do I find myself avoiding this curriculum area because I know very little about it? How active is my *idea flow* for this area of study?

Available Resources: What kinds of literature, technology, reference books, and materials do I have access to in this area? Do I know people who can give me ideas? Are there places I can go to find out more information about this subject?

Team Support: Do the teachers at my school offer ideas? Does my principal support my efforts in this area? Are there people around me I can turn to for help?

Student Needs: How fluent are my students in this area? How comfortable are they in this subject area? What do their standardized test scores show?

After completing the inventory, add together your total scores and see the next page for inventory results.

Curriculum Area	Personal Knowledge	Available Resources	Team Support	Student Needs	Total Score
Language Arts					
Social Studies					
Math					
Science					
Health					
The Arts					

Teacher as Curriculum Developer

Inventory Results

After determining your total score in each of the curriculum areas listed on the previous page, check the scoring system below to gain insight on your strengths as a curriculum developer. Following Joni's advice, work toward improvement in the area in which you have the weakest scores. Returning to the inventory and looking at your subject scores will provide you with insight on where to begin.

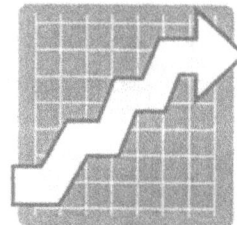

31-40 Moderate-to-High Strength

Listen to Joni, Judy, Steve, and Rhonda to reinforce many of the things you already know and to hear some new ideas that you may not have thought of yet.

21-30 Low-to-Moderate Strength

You are off to a good start developing curriculum for your children. Adopting some of the veteran teacher ideas suggested by Judy, Rhonda, Steve, and Joni can help you move to the next level.

0-20 Inadequate-to-Low Strength

You need to take a look at your performance in this subject area. Analyzing your subject scores will help you see quickly what factors are contributing to your *temporary* weakness in this area.

Teacher as Curriculum Developer

Motivation to Learn

Highly successful teachers, such as Joni, Judy, Rhonda, and Steve, often use their own hobbies and interests to motivate students. The purpose of this activity is to promote thinking as to what motivates you and how you can use that motivation as a springboard to curriculum development. Below is a three-step activity to structure your reflections. **Step 1:** Think about your hobbies and interests and how they might relate to your graded course of study. **Step 2:** List curricular areas that might relate to your area of interest. **Step 3:** Brainstorm activities you could use to teach your *interesting* objectives.

Example:

My Interest	Subject Area	Activity
Camping	Math	Estimate the mileage and time in would take to travel to designated camping location.
	Language Arts	Read a story of a family on a camping expedition.
	Social Studies	Find a Web page that lists national camping locations and resources.

Your Interest	Subject Area	Activity

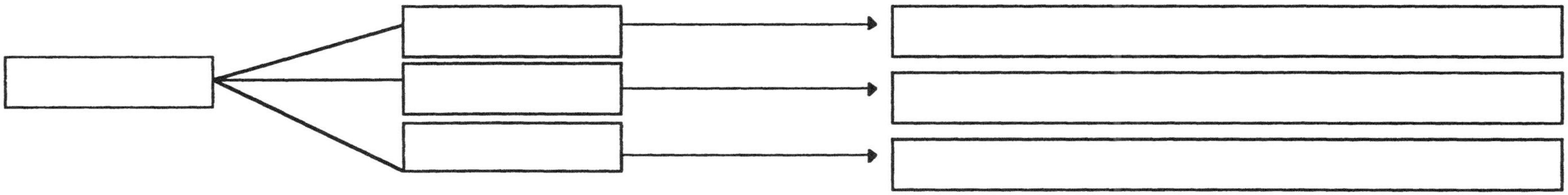

Teacher as Curriculum Developer

Lesson-Planning Survey

Lesson planning is the process whereby your professional thinking is recorded. Over time, veteran teachers develop lesson-planning methods and systems to record their thinking in efficient ways. The following list of survey questions is based on the lesson-planning ideas suggested by Joni, Judy, Rhonda, and Steve. Reviewing this list will help you develop ideas for a lesson-plan format that works well for you. Place a checkmark in each box that indicates a strategy that you incorporate in your planning.

☐ Have you asked other teachers in your school to share their lesson-planning systems?

☐ Have you tried preparing a weekly lesson-plan format on the computer?

☐ Do your lesson plans include strategies for evaluating student learning?

☐ Are your plans connected to the state's curriculum model? To your district's course of study?

☐ Are your instructional objectives stated in terms of student performance?

☐ Do your plans include a place to make notations, reflections, or comments to be remembered for next year?

☐ Are your lesson plans clear so that substitutes can follow them?

☐ Do your plans reflect diverse instructional strategies and formats, (i.e. small group, whole group, student centered, teacher centered)?

☐ Do your lesson plans provide space for listing needed materials and resources to assist in organization?

Teacher as Curriculum Developer

Sample Planning Format

Joni, Judy, Rhonda, and Steve discussed the importance of developing planning systems that help them organize time and activities across the school day and week. Specifically, they referred to creating planning documents that include recurring activities that take place on a regularly scheduled basis.

On the following page, you will find a sample planning format used by a veteran teacher to organize the week. After reviewing the format, you may want to create one of your own to assist in better managing your time and work.

It is important to recognize that the following format is a general planning document and is not a substitute for the actual lesson plans you will use in structuring specific lessons.

Sample Planning Format That You May Consider

PLEASE NOTE: Every day the schedule is . . .
9:00-9:15		Take attendance and lunch count. Do calendar activities.
9:15-11:35		Switch classes for Reading/Language Arts
11:35-12:25		Lunch/Recess
12:25-12:45		Social Studies
12:45-1:30		Math
1:30-2:00		Recess
2:00-3:00		Various Activities
3:00-3:10		Clean-up duties
3:10			Dismissal (Walkers leave first. Bussers wait in hall until bus line comes.)

MONDAY

9:15 to 9:45 Group 1 goes to special reading.
Group 2: *DOES SPELLING LESSON #_____*
9:45 to 10:15 Group 2 goes to special reading.
Group 1: *DOES SPELLING LESSON #_____*
10:15-10:40 Snack and I read:
10:40 to 11:35 Whole Group Activity: Read the story _____

11:35 -12:25 Lunch Duty (No____Yes____Time:_____)
12:25-12:45 Social Studies:

12:45-1:30 Math:

1:30-2:00 Recess Duty (No____ Yes____)
2:00-2:45 Music
2:45-3:00 Science_____
3:00-3:10 Clean-up . . . first shelf area, then cubby, then locker

---

TUESDAY

9:15 to 9:45 Group 1 goes to special reading.
Group 2: *WRITER'S WORKSHOP*
9:45 to 10:15 Group 2 goes to special reading.
Group 1: *WRITER'S WORKSHOP*
10:15-10:40 Snack and I read:
10:40 to 11:35 Literature-Based Lesson

11:35-12:25 Lunch Duty (No____Yes____Time:_____)
12:25-12:45 Social Studies:

12:45-1:30 Math:

1:30-2:00 Recess Duty (No____ Yes____)
2:00-3:00 Art . . .
3:00-3:10 Clean-up . . . first shelf area, then cubby, then locker

WEDNESDAY
9:15 to 9:45 Group 1 goes to special reading.
Group 2: *WRITER'S WORKSHOP*
9:45 to 10:15 Group 2 goes to special reading.
Group 1: *WRITER'S WORKSHOP*
10:15-10:40 Snack and I read:
10:40 to 11:35 Whole Group Activity:

11:35-12:25 Lunch Duty (No____Yes____Time:_____)
12:25-12:45 Social Studies:

12:45-1:30 Math:

1:30-2:00 Recess Duty (No____ Yes____)
2:00-3:00 Science:
3:00-3:10 Clean-up . . . first shelf area, then cubby, then locker

THURSDAY
9:15 to 9:45 Group 1 goes to special reading.
Group 2: *WRITER'S WORKSHOP*
9:45 to 10:15 Group 2 goes to special reading.
Group 1: *WRITER'S WORKSHOP*
10:15-10:40 Snack and I read:
10:40 to 11:35 Whole Group Activity:

11:35-12:25 Lunch Duty (No____Yes____Time:_____)
12:25-12:45 Social Studies:

12:45-1:30 Math:

1:30-2:00 Recess Duty (No____ Yes____)
2:00-2:40 Library
2:40-3:00 Social Science Activity
3:00-3:10 Clean-up . . . first shelf area, then cubby, then locker

FRIDAY
9:15 to 9:45 Group 1 goes to special reading.
Group 2: *GIVE THE SPELLING TEST. CHECK TO SEE WHO BROUGHT BACK HOMEWORK.*
9:45 to 10:15 Group 2 goes to special reading.
Group 1: *GIVE THE SPELLING TEST. CHECK TO SEE WHO BROUGHT BACK HOMEWORK.*
10:15-10:30 Snack and I read:
10:30 to 11:00 Language Activity MRS. SMITH WILL COME IN TO WORK WITH THE STUDENTS ON A LANGUAGE ACTIVITY.
11:00-11:35 Science
11:35-12:25 Lunch Duty (No____Yes____Time:_____)
12:25-12:45 Social Studies:

12:45-1:30 Math:

1:30-2:00 Recess Duty (No____ Yes____)
2:00-2:40 Gym teacher will pick up the students.
2:40-3:00 _____
3:00-3:10 Clean-up . . . first shelf area, then cubby, then locker

Teacher as Curriculum Developer

Advice From Joni, Judy, Rhonda, and Steve

* Buy professional books to read or to check out of the library. Read only the chapters you want to read; you do not have to read them cover to cover.

* Observe other teachers at least once a year to enrich your own curriculum.

* During your first year, concentrate and excel in *one* area of the curriculum. The following year, choose another area. This will prevent you from feeling overwhelmed.

* Join professional organizations like the National Council of Teachers of English, International Reading Association, and so on.

* "Borrow" ideas from other teachers and be willing to share your own ideas with them.

* Use quality children's literature that ties in with the concepts you are teaching.

* Talk to, plan with, and run ideas by your mentor teacher or other teachers in your school on a regular basis.

* Textbooks and teacher's manuals can be a big help to you as a beginning teacher.

References for

Teacher as Curriculum Developer

Professional Reading

Arends, R. I. (1991). *Learning to Teach* (2nd edition). McGraw-Hill.

Bacharach, Nancy, et al. (1995). *Learning Together: A Manual for Multiage Grouping*. Corwin Press.

Boone, Barbara. (1996). *Tools for Writing: Creative Writer's Workshops for Grades 2-8*. Corwin Press.

Byham, W. D. (1992). *Zapp! In Education: How Empowerment Can Improve the Quality of Instruction and Student and Teacher Satisfaction*. Fawcett Books.

Duckworth, Eleanor. (1996). *The Having of Wonderful Ideas & Other Essays on Teaching*. Teachers College Press.

Erickson, H. Lynn. (1995). *Stirring the Head, Heart, and Soul: Redefining Curriculum and Instruction*. Corwin Press.

Guthrie, Jeanne, & Perea, Karen. (1995). *Beyond Book Buddies: Interdisciplinary Teaching Across the Grades*. Corwin Press.

Hammond, M., & Collins, R. (1993). *One World, One Earth: Educating Children for Social Responsibility*. New Society.

Hovda, Ric, & Kyle, Diane. (1996). *Creating Nongraded K-3 Classrooms: Teachers' Stories and Lessons Learned*. Corwin Press.

Johnston, Christine. (1996). *Unlocking the Will to Learn*. Corwin Press.

Leaver, Betty Lou. (1997). *Teaching the Whole Class* (4th ed.). Corwin Press.

Lightfoot, Sarah Lawrence. (1985). *The Good High School: Portraits of Character and Culture*. Basic Books.

Mason, Harriet. (1996). *The Power of Storytelling: A Step-by-Step Guide to Dramatic Learning in K-12*. Corwin Press.

Nagel, Nancy. (1996). *Learning Through Real-World Problem-Solving: The Power of Intergrative Teaching.* Corwin Press.

Slavin, Robert, et al. (1996). *Every Child, Every School: Success for All.* Corwin Press.

Stone, Randi. (1997). *New Ways to Teach Using Cable Television: A Step-by-Step Guide.* Corwin Press.

Talbot, Virginia. (1997). *Teaching Reading, Writing, and Spelling: All You Need to Succeed.* Corwin Press.

Professional Organizations

International Reading Association
800 Barksdale Road
P.O. Box 8139
Newark, DE 19714-8139

National Council of Teachers of English
1111 West Kenyon Road
Urbana, IL 61801-1096
1-800-369-6283

Children's Literature

Ackerman, Karen. (1988). *Song and Dance Man.* Random House. Curriculum is everywhere and what a "lesson" Grandpa shares with his grandchildren as we follow his story of life in vaudeville.

dePaola, Tomie. (1989). *The Art Lesson.* Trumpet. Curriculum issues are abundant as you read this story of dePaola's experience with art in the elementary school.

Edwards, Julie. (1989). *The Last of the Really Great Whangdoodles.* Trophy Press. After Professor Savant tells the Potter children about the Whangdoodles, (magical creatures), their life will never been the same.

Henkes, Kevin. (1993). *Words of Stone.* Puffin Books. Blaze finds a friend for himself at a time when he desperately needs it.

Hirst, Robin. (1992). *My Place in Space.* Orchard Books. A delightful story that reinforces the many layers of geography in a fun and interesting way.

Park, Barbara. (1995). *The Kid in the Red Jacket.* Howard thinks his life is over when he learns he has to move, but then he develops a friendship with his new neighbor.

Patterson, Katherine. (1987). *Bridge to Terabithia.* A beautiful story of friendship between two young adolescents. The book is full of many issues that this age group encounters.

Polacco, Patricia. (1993). *The Bee Tree.* Philomel. One of the stories Polacco remembers from her childhood about the value of reading and learning.

Scieszka, Jon, & Smith, Lane. (1995). *Math Curse.* Viking. A hilarious story with a powerful message for all to enjoy: that learning is constant and everywhere.

Teacher as Counselor

Sometimes it is a pretty neat approach just to spend a little time observing your children, because it can be so different from what you usually see.

—Joni Edmondson

Teacher as Counselor

Warning Signs

 Steve, Judy, Rhonda, and Joni referred to warning signs about stresses that students sometimes experience. Some warning signs are listed below as a way for you to reflect on students who may need extra support. Review the list of warning signs and record students' names who may be displaying these signs.

CHARACTERISTICS   STUDENTS

1. Students who frequently act out

2. Students who fail to turn in homework

3. Students who are withdrawn

4. Students who have a constant need for the teacher's attention

5. Students with few or no friends

6. Students who are easily distracted

7. Students who constantly seek approval

8. Students who are frequently absent or tardy

9. Students who are hungry

10. Students who are angry

Please refer to The Next Step on page 41 to see what you can do to help these students.

Teacher as Counselor _____

Learning Through Observation

 Now that you have identified those students who are displaying warning signs, spend some time using a powerful tool, student observation. The following form may be used in several different ways. You may make notes as you teach a lesson, or you could invite a colleague, mentor teacher, or other professional to observe and make notes about the identified children in timed intervals, perhaps every 5 to 10 minutes. Finally, you might choose to videotape a lesson, allowing you to later reflect on the students' behavior.

Date: _____   Class: _____

Q= Inappropriate Questioning	AA= Fidgeting
IB= Inappropriate Behavior	OT= Off Task
B= Blank Stare	BC= Bothering Children
IO= Interrupting, Off Task	IT= Interrupting, On Task
DE= Disengaged	

Name:	Name:	Name:

Name:	Name:	Name:

General Comments:

Now go to the following page for a list of "next steps."

Teacher as Counselor

The Next Step

After identifying children in need and documenting the behaviors they are displaying, sometimes it is a difficult job to "take the next step." What should you, as a classroom teacher, do for a child to support his or her needs? The following list is not all-inclusive, but it can be a resource for stimulating your thinking about the next step. Remember, educators make appropriate referrals to other professionals. Involving other people is an indication of professional confidence.

_____ Consult your mentor

_____ Contact parents/family members

_____ Involve counselor

_____ Use appropriate literature

_____ Talk to colleagues

_____ Have a private conference with student

_____ Reflect through your student's journal writing

_____ Consult last year's teacher

_____ Develop peer support for the student

_____ Use class meetings

_____ Study student's past records

_____ Wait and observe changes

_____ Contact the local Children's Services

_____ Involve the school psychologist

_____ Inform principal

Teacher as Counselor

Advice From Joni, Judy, Rhonda, and Steve

* Be on the lookout for *warning signs* that are often the symptoms of deeper, more serious problems.

* Make referrals to other professionals (administrators, counselors, psychologists, social workers, etc.) in a effort to secure the help a child may need.

* Use observation as a powerful tool for collecting data on children's behavior.

* Use literature to help students process difficult situations (divorce, illness, death, etc.).

* Be careful not to get "caught in the middle" in family disputes. Do not take sides.

* Contact the home to inform parents or guardians and to secure missing information.

* Do your best to help the troubled or hurting child, but accept the limitations of what you can do in such situations.

* Thoughtfully employ journal writing to assist children in dealing with personal problems.

* Respect the child's and the family's right to privacy.

* Be descriptive rather than judgmental when speaking with parents about their child.

* Take the time to "sharpen your saw."

References for Teacher as Counselor

Professional Reading

Garcia, Cara. (1997). *Too Scared to Learn: Overcoming Academic Anxiety.* Corwin Press.

Kottler, Jeffrey, & Kottler, Ellen. (1993). *Teacher as Counselor: Developing the Helping Skills You Need.* Corwin Press.

Lasley, Thomas. (1997, April). The Missing Ingredient in Character Education, *Phi Delta Kappan*, pp. 654-655.

Martinson, Moa. (1989). *My Mother Gets Married.* Feminist Press.

Michaelis, Karen. (1993). *Reporting Child Abuse: A Guide to Mandatory Requirements for School Personnel.* Corwin Press.

Patterson, Katherine. (1995, October 15). Family Values. *New York Times Book Review*, p. 12.

Podesta, Connie. (1990). *Self-Esteem and the Six-Second Secret.* Corwin Press.

Young, B. B. (1992). *Problem-Solving Skills for Children.* Learning Tools.

Young, B. B. (1992). *The Six Vital Ingredients of Self-Esteem: How to Develop Them in Your Students.* Jalmar Press.

Children's Literature

Bunting, Eve. (1994). *Sunshine Home.* Clarion. A sensitively written book about the importance of being true and honest with our feelings.

Conly, Jane. (1993). *Crazy Lady.* HarperTrophy. This young-adult novel covers many of the issues faced by young people today (learning difficulties, peer pressures, parental alcoholism, etc.) in a sensitive way that challenges all readers. This Newbery Honor book invites the reader to consider what many young people face in their daily lives.

Creech, Sharon. (1994). *Walk Two Moons*. HarperCollins. This 1995 Newbery winner is an utterly delightful journey through a thirteen-year-old's life as she and her girlfriend struggle with some tough challenges.

Krementz, Jill. (1988). *How It Feels When a Parent Dies*. Knopf Press. Krementz does an outstanding job of helping the reader empathize with the issue of losing a parent as she interviews children who have actually experienced such a loss.

Krisher, Trudy. (1992). *Kathy's Hats*. Albert Whitman. In this beautifully written picture book, the reader gets a glimpse into the pain of childhood cancer.

Teacher as Evaluator

The question we must always ask ourselves is: "What is really going to measure the learning that's taking place?"

-Steve Huff

Teacher as Evaluator

Completing the Picture

It is important to look at students holistically when evaluating them. Some students will be stronger on different tasks, depending on individual learning styles. To form a more complete picture of a child's ability, it is important to look at more than one piece of the puzzle. Represented below are a few puzzle pieces you may want to add to your evaluation plan. Place a check mark next to the pieces that you currently use to evaluate your students, or create new pieces of your own. Remember, the more pieces you have, the more detailed the final picture.

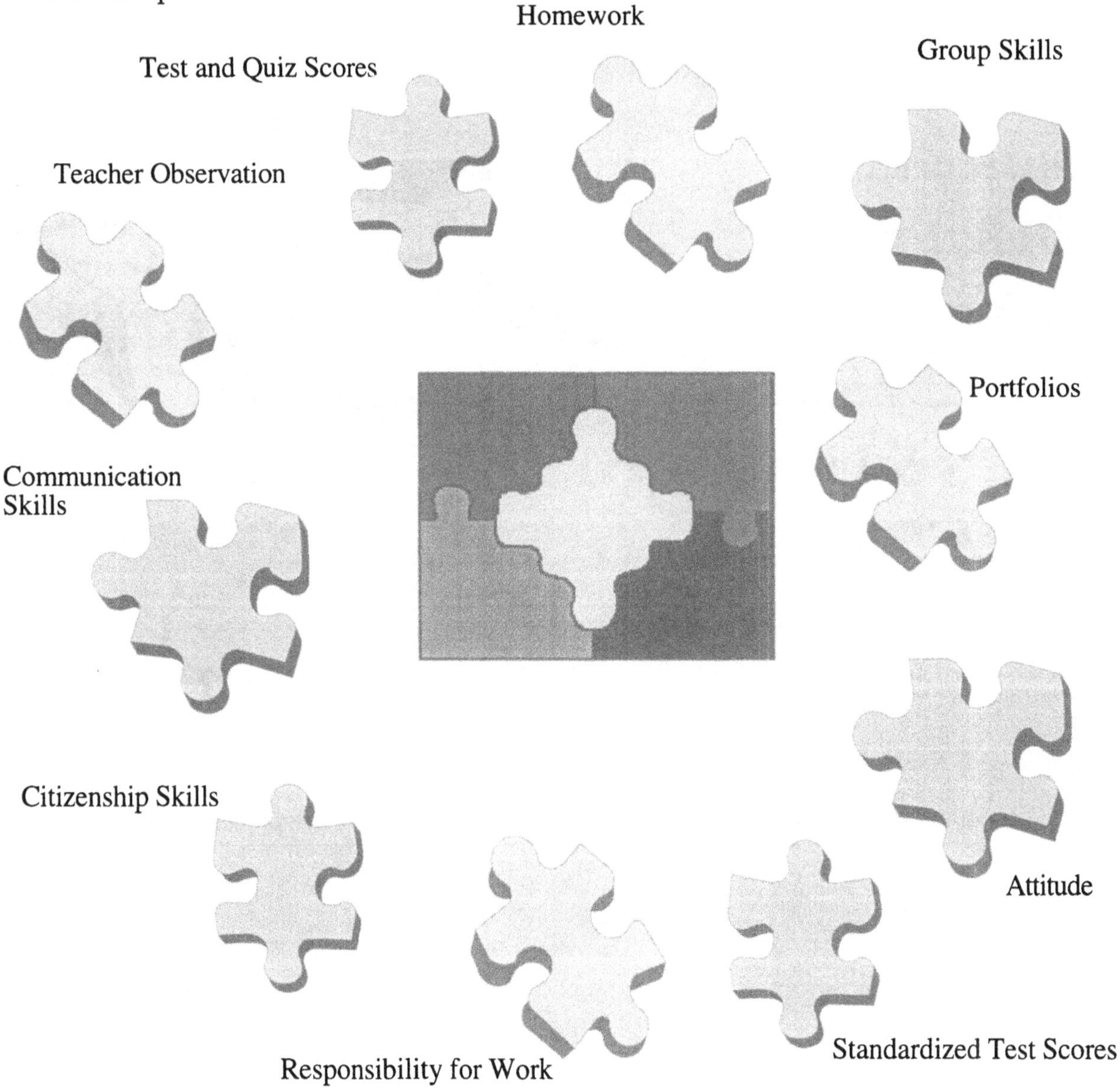

- Homework
- Test and Quiz Scores
- Group Skills
- Teacher Observation
- Portfolios
- Communication Skills
- Citizenship Skills
- Attitude
- Responsibility for Work
- Standardized Test Scores

46

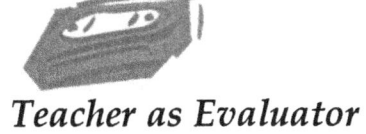

Teacher as Evaluator

Family Conference Tips

- Families want to hear positive things about their children!

- Talk about both academic and social skills.

- Consider beginning your conference by saying, "Tell me about your child."

- Share your goals for the child with the family. Ask them, "What do you think?" and "What would you like to add?" The families will appreciate being involved in these decisions.

- For the first years that you hold conferences, jot down notes on each child in an individual folder ahead of time, so you do not struggle for something to comment on.

- Create a comfortable atmosphere for the families. Prepare a newsletter for them to read while they wait, provide nice seats in the hallway, and perhaps even offer refreshments. (These can be ones the kids made!)

- Hang a schedule in the hallway so families are aware of the time constraints.

- Spend more time listening than talking.

- Make monthly or bimonthly calls to families, so when conference time arrives, they are not so surprised at what you have to say.

- Keep your expectations for each child handy.

- If you do not have students' work displayed in the room or hallway, have some work samples available for families to see.

- Offer the families one thing they could do at home to help their child, and ask them for one thing you can do to help their child at school.

Teacher as Evaluator

Planning the Path

Remember that Judy discussed the importance of internalizing your overall objectives: "What do I want my children to know?" Now that you have reflected on the pieces that can create an evaluation plan, take some time to develop a specific evaluation plan for a project your children are currently working on or a unit you are teaching. Complete the following plan to help you develop a strong evaluation plan for your children's work.

What do I want my children to know?
___
___
___

What evaluation strategies will I use to determine if these goals have been met?
___
___
___

What modifications will I make for students with special needs?
___
___
___

How will I involve the students in the evaluation process?
___
___
___

How will I communicate students' progress to their families?
___
___
___

What do I need to do to get ready?
___
___
___

Teacher as Evaluator

Advice From Joni, Judy, Rhonda, and Steve

* Have high expectations for your students. Focus on quality, not quantity.

* Make appropriate adjustments for special-needs students.

* Designate a time each day when you can observe your students and take notes on them.

* Make an "I'm invisible" badge when observing.

* Hang charts in the room that list the requirements for your grades. Let the students help in setting these requirements.

* Focus on the positive aspects of your students' work when you evaluate, but be clear about where improvement needs to occur.

* Be sure to assess your students in several different ways, not only on tests and quizzes.

* Let the students evaluate themselves now and then.

* Let the students evaluate each other periodically.

* Remember, you do not have to record every single paper in your grade book!

* As you decide on fair and consistent techniques for evaluating your students, recall Steve's words: "What is really going to measure the learning that's taking place?"

# References for
Teacher as Evaluator

Professional Reading

Batzle, J. (1992). *Portfolio Assessment and Evaluation.* Creative Teaching Press.

Burz, Helen, & Marshall, Kit. (1997). *Performance-Based Curriculum for Language Arts: From Knowing to Showing.* Corwin Press.

Burz, Helen, & Marshall, Kit. (1996). *Performance-Based Curriculum for Mathematics: From Knowing to Showing.* Corwin Press.

Burz, Helen, & Marshall, Kit. (1997). *Performance-Based Curriculum for Science: From Knowing to Showing.* Corwin Press.

Burz, Helen, & Marshall, Kit. (1997). *Performance-Based Curriculum for Social Studies: From Knowing to Showing.* Corwin Press.

Goodman, K., Bird, L., & Goodman, Y. (1992). *The Whole Language Catalog: Supplement on Authentic Assessment.* Macmillan/McGraw-Hill.

Hart, D. (1994). *Authentic Assessment: A Handbook for Educators.* Addison-Wesley.

Jasmine, J. (1993). *Portfolios and Other Assessments.* Teacher Created Materials.

McLean, James, & Lockwood, Robert. (1996). *Why We Assess Students--And How: The Competing Measures of Student Performance.* Corwin Press.

Tierney, R., Carter, M., & Desai, L. (1991). *Portfolio Assessment in the Reading-Writing Classroom.* Christopher-Gordon.

Children's Literature

Condra, Estelle. (1994). *See the Ocean.* Ideals Children's Books. There are many ways to "see" things as Nellie teaches her family.

Scieszka, Jon. (1989). *The True Story of the Three Little Pigs!* Viking Kestrel. This hilarious book teaches educators to consider different perspectives before making evaluatory decisions.

Shaw, Charles. (1947). *It Looked Like Spilt Milk.* Harper & Row. The message of this simple picture book is that when evaluating, it is critical to look at the child from multiple perspectives.

Young, Ed. (1992). *Seven Blind Mice.* Philomel. It is important to see the "whole" picture when evaluating children's learning.

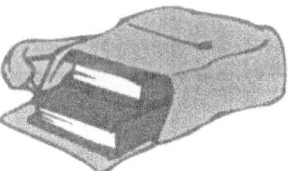

Teacher as Diversity Specialist

As Sarah Lawrence Lightfoot reminds us, "every child brings a gift to school, but so often that gift is left at the door." Beginning teachers need to make sure each child's gift makes it to the classroom to be discovered and celebrated.

-Tricia Hart

Teacher as Diversity Specialist

Gift List

In reference to Sarah Lawrence Lightfoot's belief that every child brings a gift to school, the purpose of this activity is to help you prevent that gift from being "left at the door." In order to help you focus on your students and their gifts, complete the following chart. Gifts could include a sense of humor, being a storyteller, an attitude of kindness, athletic ability, and so on. If you cannot easily identify a particular child's gift, challenge yourself to find it. When you do, record it here with special emphasis!

Child's Name	Gift

Teacher as Diversity Specialist

Self-Evaluation

This activity is designed to help you take inventory of your use of instructional strategies that can help meet individual student's needs. Please read the specific strategy and check F (Frequently), O (Occasionally), or N (Never) to indicate the frequency of usage in your classroom.

	F	**O**	**N**
Cooperative learning	—	—	—
Small-group work	—	—	—
Peer teaching	—	—	—
Remediation	—	—	—
Extension activities	—	—	—
Conferencing with students	—	—	—
Use of technology	—	—	—
Teacher observation	—	—	—
Student choice of assignments	—	—	—
Alternate use of visual, auditory, and kinesthetic strategies	—	—	—

Scoring:
Give yourself 5 points for every **Frequently**.
Give yourself 3 points for every **Occasionally**.
Give yourself 0 points for every **Never**.

- 0-10   Needs improvement!
- 10-25   Not too bad!
- 25-35   Keep up the fabulous work!

My total score is:

Teacher as Diversity Specialist

Celebrating Diversity

As a diversity specialist, it is important to recognize and celebrate the things that make us unique and special. At some point, early in the year, have the children in your class complete an activity like the one that follows this page. You may also want to create an activity of your own that allows you to discover what each of your children feels makes him or her special and unique. Include yourself when gathering this information, so that you can talk to your children about how you share your own gifts and talents. Discuss each person's uniqueness and how it contributes to the group. Develop ways throughout the year to incorporate children's gifts in classroom activities.

Teacher as Diversity Specialist _____

I Am Special

My name is _____.

My birthday is _____ and I am ___ years old.

My favorite thing to eat is _____.

I do not like when people _____.

What sets me apart from everybody else is the fact that I can/am_____.

The following people live in my house:

    __mom   __grandma
    __dad   __grandpa
    __stepmom   __cat
    __stepdad   __dog
    __brothers   __other pet
    __sisters   __uncle
    __stepsisters   __aunt
    __stepbrothers __ other person

Of these people, I am closest to _____.

When I grow up, I would like to _____.

Teacher as Diversity Specialist

Advice From Joni, Judy, Rhonda, and Steve

* Become aware of the many differences in your classroom.

* Ensure that all students feel welcome in your classroom.

* Be careful *not* to compare students to each other.

* Know that *you* set the tone in the classroom--if you accept individual differences, so will your students.

* Take one or two professional days each school year to observe teachers in other classrooms. What do they do?

* Allow students the freedom to work in a style and pace that is successful for them.

* Use quality children's literature to accommodate individual differences.

* Invite resource people in to speak to your students.

* Have students fill out surveys to help you learn about their needs.

* Take into consideration visual, auditory, and kinesthetic learners. Try your best to adapt lessons to fit the needs of these learners.

* Be ready to extend lessons for some students and simplify for others.

* Acknowledge that you will not be able to meet every child's needs your first year of teaching.

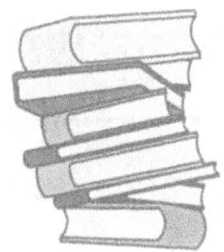

References for
Teacher as Diversity Specialist

Professional Reading

Aefsky, Fern. (1995). *Inclusion Confusion: A Guide to Educating Students With Exceptional Needs.* Corwin Press.

Bishop, R. (1992). *Multicultural Literature for Children: Making Informed Choices.* Christopher-Gordon.

Davidman, L. (1994). *Teaching With a Multicultural Perspective: A Practical Guide.* Longman.

Harris, V. J. (Ed.). *Teaching Multicultural Literature.* Christopher-Gordon.

Kottler, Ellen. (1994). *Children With Limited English: Teaching Strategies for the Regular Classroom.* Corwin Press.

McEwan, Elaine K. (1997). *The ADHD Checklist for Teachers.* Corwin Press.

Rong, Xue Lan, & Preissle, Judith. (1997). *Educating Immigrant Students: What We Need to Know to Meet the Challenges.* Corwin Press.

Sims, R. (1982). *Shadow and Substance.* National Council of Teachers of English.

Wood, J. W. (1991). *Adapting Instruction for Mainstreamed and At-Risk Students.* Merrill.

Kids on the Block, Inc.
9385-C Gerwig Lane
Columbia, MD 21046-1583
1-800-368-KIDS
Kids on the Block is a national program established in 1977 that offers educational awareness programs on sensitivity, awareness, and acceptance of differences.

Touch Math
Touch Math Resource Center Set
Innovative Learning Concepts
6760 Corporate Drive
Colorado Springs, CO 80919-1999

A World of Ideas With Bill Moyers
Videocassette: 3-tape set
Order #MYS-76021
Audiotape: 3-tape set
Order #MYS-76901

Order Information
Purdue University
Instructional Media Center
1532 Stewart Center
West Lafayette, IN 47907-1532

Children's Literature

Fleming, Virginia. (1993). *Be Good to Eddie Lee*. Philomel. A message about kindness is internalized by a young girl, which makes a difference in Eddie Lee's day. Eddie Lee has Down's Syndrome.

Hamanaka, Shelia. (1994). *All the Colors of the Race*. Morrow. A beautifully written and illustrated poem with an important message for all children to experience.

Kindersley, Barnabas, & Kindersley, Anabel. (1995). *Children Just Like Me*. Dorling Kindersley. An exquisite presentation of the theme that children all around the world value the same things: family, clothing, special foods, cultural identity, and so on.

McKissack, Patricia. (1988). *Mirandy and Brother Wind*. Knopf. Hard work, determination, and perseverance pays off for Mirandy and Ezel in the Junior Cake Walk.

Mitchell, Margaree. (1993). *Uncle Jed's Barbershop*. Simon & Schuster. A powerful book about family love and the value of persistence.

Philbrick, Rodman. (1993). *Freak the Mighty*. Blue Sky Press. This young adult novel captivates the reader as Kevin, a junior high student with a physical disability, develops a deep friendship with Max, a junior high student with a mental disability.

Rylant, Cynthia. (1991). *Appalachia*. Harcourt Brace Jovanovich. As the reader travels through this masterfully written picture book, respect for the Appalachian culture develops.

Say, Allen. (1993). *Grandfather's Journey*. Houghton Mifflin. This 1994 Caldecott winner very honestly portrays the torn feeling of immigrants as they struggle with love and allegiances for two cultures.

Walter, Mildred. (1995). *The Girl on the Outside*. Scholastic Publications. An exciting historical novel that tells the story of two young girls living in the time of the beginning of school integration.

The Joys of Teaching

When there comes a time I stop learning, that will be the time for me to stop teaching.

-Judy Eggemeier

The Joys of Teaching

Shining Star

Joni, Judy, Rhonda, and Steve believe their own teaching careers have been strongly affected by certain teachers they had while growing up. Think back to your own school days. Who was your very favorite teacher? Why did you like him or her so much? What qualities did this particular teacher possess that inspired you? Make a list of some of these qualities below.

My very favorite teacher was _____.

He or she taught _____ grade.

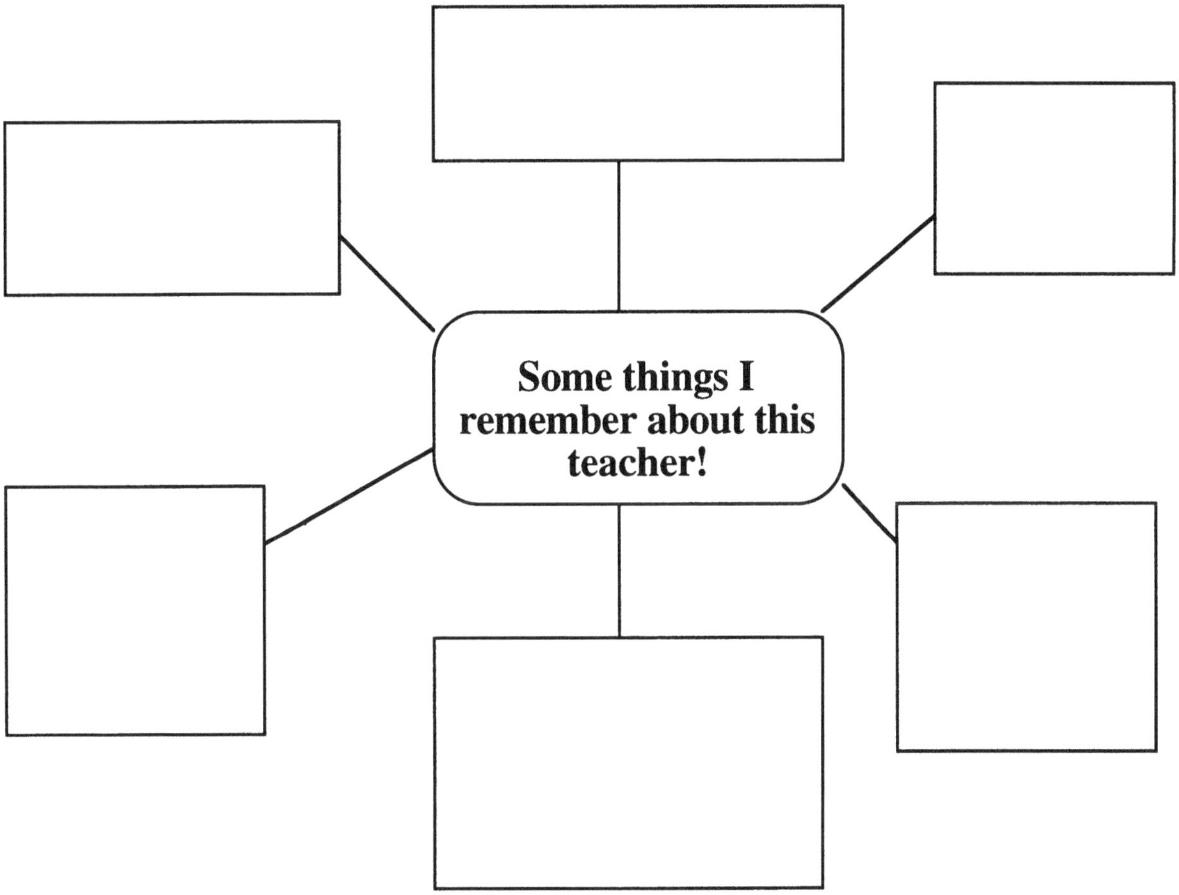

Some things I remember about this teacher!

Great! Now reread the boxes. Have you carried on any of these traditions? Circle the qualities that you have modeled in your own classroom. Shade in the boxes with the behaviors that you would like to adopt in the future.

The Joys of Teaching

Secrets of Success

In the final program, Joni, Judy, Rhonda, and Steve were asked to describe the *secret of their success*. After reviewing their answers, fill in the final space with a description of your own secret of success. If you feel you have had a less than successful time overall, focus on the smaller successes you did have. Describe what worked in those situations, and it may give you valuable insight into your future success.

JONI: I get to know the background of my students, emotionally, socially, and academically.

JUDY: I look at each day as a privilege.

RHONDA: I believe that school should not be a preparation for life; it should *be* life.

STEVE: I don't concentrate so much on facts. Parents don't care how much you know. They want to know how much you care about their children.

-------YOUR SECRET OF SUCCESS-------

_____ : _____

_____

_____

The Joys of Teaching

Summer Contract

Joni, Judy, Rhonda, and Steve all discussed the importance of using summer vacation to renew themselves in different ways. Although you are likely to find yourself frequently reflecting on your first year and planning for your second, be sure you also find time to pursue those activities that you find personally renewing. To help you identify and commit to those activities, complete the following contract prior to the last day of school. Remember, contracts should not be broken . . .

I, _____, hereby agree to take it easy on myself this upcoming summer break. During this vacation, I promise to have fun and take part in the following NON-SCHOOL activities:

1.

2.

3.

I understand that too much reflection on the past year may cause high stress levels and result in a very unpleasant summertime for me and those around me. I know that the first year of the teaching profession is a difficult one, and Joni, Judy, Rhonda, and Steve have acknowledged making mistakes during this time. I have learned from the mistakes I made, and I have already begun to improve as an educator.

So, keeping the above in mind, I vow to relax and take a break. I agree to complete my three "oxygen-mask" activities regularly!

_____
signature

_____
date

The Joys of Teaching

A Year in Review

Joni, Judy, Rhonda, and Steve all described ways in which they have grown since they first began teaching. Think back through your first year of teaching. How have you changed or grown, and what have you learned from this experience? Has it been a positive year? What will you do differently the next time around? What experience has had the greatest impact on you? Briefly reflect on these prompts and record your answers below.

The Joys of Teaching

Advice From Joni, Judy, Rhonda, and Steve

* Surround yourself with people who love teaching rather than those who bring you down.

* Do what works for you in the classroom.

* Continue to develop outside interests.

* Develop a thematic unit to teach that excites you.

* Continue to develop new goals.

* Always look for new ways to do things.

* Relax, read, and spend time alone or with people you enjoy.

* Attend some of the extracurricular activities in which students in your classroom participate.

* Model some of your teaching strategies after your favorite teacher.

* Always come back to "what is best for the children I teach."

# References for
The Joys of Teaching

Professional Reading

Bogue, E. (1991). *A Journey of the Heart: The Call to Teaching.* Phi Delta Kappa.

Canfield, J., & Hansen, M. (1993). *Chicken Soup for the Soul: 101 Stories to Open the Heart and Rekindle the Spirit.* Health Communications.

Henry, Eric, et al. (1995). *To Be a Teacher: Voices From the Classroom.* Corwin Press.

Johnson, L. (1992). *My Posse Don't Do Homework.* St. Martin's.

Ladson-Billings, G. (1994). *The Dreamkeepers: Successful Teachers of African American Children.* Jossey-Bass.

Ryan, K., & Cooper, J. (1988). *Those Who Can, Teach.* Houghton Mifflin.

Zehm, Stanley, & Kottler, Jeffrey. (1993). *On Being a Teacher: The Human Dimension.* Corwin Press.

Children's Literature

Dakos, Kalli. (1990). *If You're Not Here, Please Raise Your Hand.* Macmillan. The title alone indicates that this wonderful collection of poems is written from a teacher's perspective.

Dr. Seuss. (1990). *Oh, the Places You'll Go!* Random House. A fun, inspirational book about embarking on any career, particularly pertinent for educators.

Houston, Gloria. (1992). *My Great-Aunt Arizona.* HarperCollins. An inspirational picture book about the impact educators make in the lives of the children they teach over many generations.

Konigsburg, E. (1996). *The View From Saturday.* Atheneum. The 1997 Newbery winner is a story about a teacher who views her diverse group of learners with an open and supportive attitude.

Winch, John. (1993). *The Old Man Who Loved to Sing*. Scholastic. Teachers can no longer teach in isolation; they must depend on their professional community to keep on "singing," even when times get tough.

CORWIN
PRESS

The Corwin Press logo — a raven striding across an open book — represents the happy union of courage and learning. We are a professional-level publisher of books and journals for K–12 educators, and we are committed to creating and providing resources that embody these qualities. Corwin's motto is "Success for All Learners."

In compliance with GPSR, should you have any concerns about the safety of this product, please advise: International Associates Auditing & Certification Limited The Black Church, St Mary's Place, Dublin 7, D07 P4AX Ireland EUAR@ie.ia-net.com

www.ingramcontent.com/pod-product-compliance
Lightning Source LLC
Chambersburg PA
CBHW082246300426
44110CB00039B/2450